SandCastle™

First Rhymes

Thad and His Dad

Mary Elizabeth Salzmann

Consulting Editor, Diane Craig, M.A./Reading Specialist

Publishing Company

Published by ABDO Publishing Company, 4940 Viking Drive, Edina, Minnesota 55435.

Copyright © 2006 by Abdo Consulting Group, Inc. International copyrights reserved in all countries. No part of this book may be reproduced in any form without written permission from the publisher. SandCastle™ is a trademark and logo of ABDO Publishing Company.

Printed in the United States.

Credits
Edited by: Pam Price
Curriculum Coordinator: Nancy Tuminelly
Cover and Interior Design and Production: Mighty Media
Photo Credits: AbleStock, Eyewire Images, Rubberball Productions

Library of Congress Cataloging-in-Publication Data

Salzmann, Mary Elizabeth, 1968-
    Thad and his dad / Mary Elizabeth Salzmann.
        p. cm. -- (First rhymes)
    Includes index.
    ISBN 1-59679-537-9 (hardcover)
    ISBN 1-59679-538-7 (paperback)
        1. English language--Rhyme--Juvenile literature. I. Title. II. Series.
PE1517.S3595 2006
808.1--dc22

                                                                    2005048802

SandCastle™ books are created by a professional team of educators, reading specialists, and content developers around five essential components that include phonemic awareness, phonics, vocabulary, text comprehension, and fluency. All books are written, reviewed, and leveled for guided reading and early intervention reading, and designed for use in shared, guided, and independent reading and writing activities to support a balanced approach to literacy instruction.

Let Us Know

After reading the book, SandCastle would like you to tell us your stories about reading. What is your favorite page? Was there something hard that you needed help with? Share the ups and downs of learning to read. We want to hear from you! To get posted on the ABDO Publishing Company Web site, send us e-mail at:

sandcastle@abdopub.com

SandCastle Level: Beginning

-ad

brad

dad

glad

lad

pad

This is a .

Here is my  .

She feels  .

He is a .

This is a .

The brad is sharp.

Lisa hugs her dad.

Tammy is glad.

This lad is sitting.

The pad is yellow.

Thad and His Dad

Thad is a good lad.

16

Thad the good lad
loves his dad.

Thad the good lad got a big pad from his dad.

Thad the good lad
drew a brad
on the pad
he got from his dad.

"The brad
you drew on the pad
is not bad!"
said Thad's dad.

That made Thad
the good lad glad!

About SandCastle™

A professional team of educators, reading specialists, and content developers created the SandCastle™ series to support young readers as they develop reading skills and strategies and increase their general knowledge. The SandCastle™ series has four levels that correspond to early literacy development in young children. The levels are provided to help teachers and parents select the appropriate books for young readers.

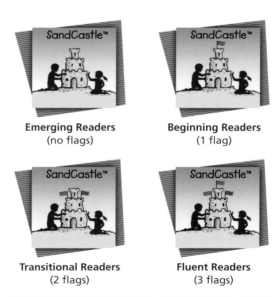

Emerging Readers
(no flags)

Beginning Readers
(1 flag)

Transitional Readers
(2 flags)

Fluent Readers
(3 flags)

These levels are meant only as a guide. All levels are subject to change.

To see a complete list of SandCastle™ books and other nonfiction titles from ABDO Publishing Company, visit **www.abdopub.com** or contact us at:
4940 Viking Drive, Edina, Minnesota 55435 • 1-800-800-1312 • fax: 1-952-831-1632